The World We Know

The Impact of Perception and Empathy on Our Shared Reality

Sheryle Gillihan

For my husband Michael and our daughters.

In all my versions of reality and fantasy,
you are my everything.

Acknowledgements

Michael Gillihan, as my partner in all things your support has always been invaluable. You help me rise as my best self and are there to catch me and help me when I falter.

Alli and Max Gillihan, my sweet girls, thank you for supporting and encouraging me even in my weakest moments.

Christina Dodson, my mother who in this story was very tough on me. Her perspective helped shape me.

Don Williams, your self-publishing class has been a game changer. Thank you for your encouragement.

Roy Odhner, Megan Mullin, & Mike Fowler, I couldn't have done this without your support.

Brooke Lively, thank you for being my first editor.

Sanger Smith, your book and your insights on authoring a book have been instrumental.

EO Visionaries Forum (past and present), thank you for your friendship and contributing to my growth.

Table of Contents

"The pure and simple truth is rarely pure and never simple."

OSCAR WILDE

Introduction

In our daily lives, we navigate an intricate web of perceptions, beliefs, and experiences that collectively form our understanding of reality — or, as I refer to in this book, 'The World We Know.'

This world, however, is far more complex and malleable than it appears at first glance. 'The World We Know' explores the facets of perspective, truth, reality, and humanity in our ever-evolving world.

This book touches on topics of immigration, war, violence, abuse, and suicide. If even the hint of these subjects is too much, please feel free to set the book aside for another day.

A Personal Note
from The Author

This book has been brewing inside me for what feels like an eternity. I used to question whether I had any right to share these thoughts. After all, I'm not a certified psychologist or a renowned academic researcher. The message in these pages may not be groundbreaking or entirely unique. But as I continue my journey of self-discovery, unraveling my worldview and seeking personal growth, I feel an undeniable urge to put pen to paper.

The topics I delve into in 'The World We Know' emerged from various sources including my experiences in leadership training, as well as a life-altering crisis that left me repeating the phrase, "The truth is only what is believed." In this moment of my shattered reality, I was transported back to a five-year-old version of myself, lost in a haze of confusion.

I've been dealing with deep-rooted PTSD for more than 40 years. While seeking help, I discovered the kaleidoscope of thinking errors and irrational beliefs that colored my perception of life and tainted my interactions with others. I had no idea that my pain had caused such cascading effects that perpetuated into adulthood. I had forced it out of my mind or so I thought, but my demons lingered, hiding in waiting like predators waiting for the opportune moment.

These cognitive roadblocks, the sticking points that held me back and prevented me from fully embracing life's wonders, tie directly into the themes explored in this book. The loudest of these inner voices holds onto this belief:

"I am not important enough to be believed."

It is maddening and fascinating how our beliefs can affect our perception of the world and our subsequent behaviors.

With the slightest trigger, my perspective shifted, and the seemingly perfect reality I had created shattered. Those self-deprecating views I had silently endured and tried to conceal became all-encompassing, echoing relentlessly in my mind.

So, how did I find my way back to a semblance of normalcy? It took considerable support, but I can confidently say that I am not merely back to normal — I have started to surpass it. Through ongoing support, self-work, and introspection, I have become a better version of myself, forged in the crucible of my crisis.

Parts of the narrative in this book are deeply personal and offer a raw, sometimes painful, testimony. I share these chapters of my tangented thoughts, these struggles and challenges, because I know that I'm not the only one wrestling with these profound questions. There are parts of my story, though, that I'm at peace with leaving behind. I've come to terms with these chapters, and I no longer feel the need to revisit their reality, not even for the brief, painful moment it takes to commit them to paper.

I'm grateful for your willingness to join in exploring our shared reality. You are graciously providing your time and attention to these pages, and that is a gift. I hope that you find value, as I did, in the topics explored throughout 'The World We Know.'

This book was born from a deep desire to understand the intricacies of perception, empathy, and the power of diverse perspectives.

In the following chapters, we will delve into the depths of human experience, traversing the landscapes of perception, belief, and the intricate interplay between our personal truths and the collective reality we inhabit. Through personal anecdotes, thought-provoking insights, and the wisdom of philosophers, scientists, and visionaries, we will embark on a journey that challenges our preconceived notions and expands our understanding of 'The World We Know.'

The structure of this book is designed to guide you through a tapestry of ideas, each chapter building upon the previous one to create a rich mosaic of understanding. We will explore the malleability of reality, the duality of truth, the influence of society on our worldview, and the importance of embracing diverse perspectives. We will navigate the pitfalls of echo chambers, immerse ourselves in cultural experiences, and learn to embrace the unknown with courage and curiosity.

I hope that as you engage with the ideas presented in these pages, you will embark on your journey of self-discovery and growth. I sincerely wish that this book catalyzes transformation, igniting a spark within you to question, explore, and challenge the boundaries of your understanding.

I invite you to approach this book with an open heart and mind. Allow the words and ideas to resonate within you, sparking new insights and igniting your curiosity. Where you find discomfort, allow yourself time and space to explore it for understanding. May you find inspiration in the stories shared, the perspectives explored, and the calls to action that emerge from these pages.

This book doesn't offer neat solutions; instead, it serves as an invitation—an exploration into the depths of our understanding of ourselves and others. I believe that by engaging in this exploration, we can create positive change in ourselves, our communities, and the world at large.

Thank you for your courage to embrace self-discovery and a quest for greater empathy and awareness.

With gratitude and anticipation,

CHAPTER 1

The Malleability of Reality

What is reality? You need to delve into philosophy, science, and human cognition to answer this. It's a question that has puzzled thinkers for centuries, from the ancient Greek philosopher Plato to modern-day cognitive neuroscientist. At its core, reality is subjective, shaped by your individual experiences, cultures, and mental constructs.

How does that show up in our lives? Imagine you grew up in a bustling city, while your sibling grew up in a small town. Your perceptions of reality will differ drastically despite sharing the same genetic material. This example might resonate with you, even if you haven't been born in different places.

Perhaps, you and your siblings were born decades apart. You not only have different societal experiences, you may also seem to have different parents even if you're raised by the same mother and father. This illustrates the inherent malleability of reality despite the facts of a situation remaining the same, showcasing how it bends and morphs under the weight of unique experiences and circumstances. It serves as a reminder that your perception of the world is shaped not only by objective truths but also by the subjective lenses through which you view and interpret your life.

Your brain is a meaning-making machine. It possesses an extraordinary capacity to construct meaning out of vast amounts of information, "to make sense of the information bombarding us every day," Susan David astutely highlights in her book Emotional Agility. Your brain diligently sifts through the raw sensory input, piecing together fragments to weave a coherent narrative that aligns with your personal understanding of the world — your perceived 'reality.'

Consider the sheer magnitude of information your senses absorb — a symphony of sights, sounds, smells, tastes, and tactile sensations. Yet, it's not enough for your brain to merely process this data objectively. It seeks patterns, connections, and context, striving to transform the raw input into a cohesive and meaningful story that you can comprehend and navigate.

In this remarkable cognitive process, your brain acts as a skilled storyteller, drawing upon past experiences, learned knowledge, cultural influences, and personal biases. It molds the incoming stimuli into a narrative that resonates with your unique perspective, constructing a subjective reality that feels coherent and sensible to you based on your pre-existing view of the world.

Familiar patterns can produce an instinctual feeling of trust and comfort. From a business perspective whether you're closing a new sale or choosing a service provider for your home, think about the ease and comfort of relationships formed from referral-based conversations in comparison to cold calling. There is nothing wrong with these practices for establishing trust. In fact, there is great strength in the ability to foster these relationships.

However, our brains can also send false alarms. This is where unfamiliar settings can trigger fear, distrust, or opposition. This gut reaction can be unwarranted yet often trusted. This can hinder your creativity, prevent you from appreciating new experiences, and can lead you to seek out confirmation bias that your comfortable stance is valid and warranted.

Let's talk about how this helps or hurts from a business perspective. Encountering betrayal and disappointment in unfamiliar scenarios has caused me to struggle as a leader. "How did I miss the signs?" It not only causes me to question my judgment and shift the patterns of perceived trust, but it has on several occasions led to therapy to deal with grief, as if I had lost a loved one. It changes me and thus, my future experiences. It could very easily hold me back and take a "did that and it failed" approach.

While I like to quote Einstein's definition of insanity, I must admit that my personality errs on the side of madness and perhaps that's why I'm an entrepreneur. I will do the same thing over and over again because the reality is that in most cases, it's never exactly the same and it takes persistence to achieve success.

There are hundreds of thousands of books teaching us the "right things" and they contain valuable lessons to log into our pattern libraries. I know, I'm an avid reader. However, none of those books can control all of the conditions when employing those practices. Not only do we need to be aware of the unique conditions, we must also accept that there are perspectives beyond your knowledge and beyond our control. When the vision I create fits with your reality, and those patterns of trust are finally forged then, I've graduated from insane to innovative. The world we know converges.

Your self-created reality is not fixed or unchangeable. It's fluid and adaptable, continually evolving as you encounter new information and revise your understanding of the world. Your Aha! moments are catalysts that spark insightful shifts in your perspective, opening the doors to new narratives of understanding and igniting the transformative power within you.

The same set of circumstances can be perceived and interpreted differently by different individuals, as their brains apply distinct filters and lenses based on their unique backgrounds, beliefs, and experiences.

The narratives your brain creates become your reality, shaping your thoughts, emotions, and actions.

Understanding the intricacies of this process invites you to reflect on the power and limitations of your perception. It encourages you to approach the diverse perspectives of others with curiosity and empathy, recognizing that their reality, though different from yours, is just as valid and meaningful to them. By embracing the malleability of your constructed realities, you open yourself to a richer tapestry of understanding and foster a greater appreciation for the diverse ways in which you experience the world.

> *"Your ambition should be to get as much
> life out of living as you possibly can, as
> much enjoyment, as much interest, as much
> experience, as much understanding."*

ELEANOR ROOSEVELT

An Immersive Quest for Cultural Insights

Another fascinating perspective on the malleability of reality comes from the field of anthropology and ethnography. These researchers immerse themselves into foreign cultures. Bronislaw Malinowski, a renowned anthropologist and ethnologist, wrote it is vital to "grasp the native's point of view, his relation to life, to realize his vision of his world."

Anthropologists, who are deeply immersed into the vibrant fabric of diverse cultures, attain profound understanding by embracing both the insider's view (emic) and the outsider's perspective (etic).

By witnessing people's daily routines, experiencing their way of living firsthand, and delving into what holds deep meaning in their lives, the researchers unlock a comprehensive understanding of their world. This holistic and immersive approach enables researchers to grasp the intricate nuances and fosters a comprehensive appreciation for the complexity of human experiences.

While this impacts our anthropological understanding of the human experience, and also helps with missionaries immersing themselves into a rural village, there are current examples of how this can impact progress.

What's in the Water

In one story told by Amina J. Mohammed, a group of well-intentioned philanthropists donated to build a well in a small village in Africa to provide clean water. The women of this region walked for hours to get water from the river. The river water was red and causing health problems in the community. In order to build this well the philanthropist needed to gain approval from the government. With all the approvals in place the well was built. However, two years after the project was complete, a group visited the village and saw that the women were still walking to the river for water. "Why don't you use the water in the well?" To that very simple question the elders replied, "That water does not look like our water, and because it was put in by the government we don't know what is in it."

Strong beliefs can cause strong opposition to progress. Despite the intentions of those providing access to clean water, they failed to understand the realities of this community and failed to create bridges of trust and understanding. Consider this case study and this story. Where are you ineffective at fostering the progress you want to see and why might that be the case? This story might also prompt you to evaluate where and how you donate to ensure your gift creates the impact you desire.

Appreciation: A Path, Not a Destination

While appreciating the intricate tapestry of human experiences is crucial for nurturing empathy and bridging divides, we must remember that understanding doesn't always equate to acceptance or positive affirmation.

Take my story, for instance. My roots are deeply entrenched in Filipino culture. Born to an unmarried mother and a U.S. airman who didn't even know of my existence, my early life was, to put it lightly, unconventional. It wasn't until I was six that my parents married, using my existence as leverage to chase the elusive American Dream. Suddenly, I found myself transformed into a military child in the U.S., thrust into a world of surprising delights and opportunities - a concept alien to my homeland. From public schooling and healthcare to the 'common' marvel of indoor plumbing, these were my newfound abundances. And oh, how I can laugh now, recalling my Ariel-esque bewilderment at using a fork for the first time, a memento of a past where eating with my hands was the norm.

My own upbringing, a blend of diverse cultures and circumstances, shaped me in a very particular way. As a female, I was taught to be subservient. As a military child, obedience was demanded. As an immigrant, gratitude was expected. Striving for perfection became my reality, a reality tainted with the belief of inevitable failure and the constant need to apologize for my existence. The fear, the shame, the hope of one day being 'good enough' became my companions.

I lived with these notions because, as a child, I didn't know any different. My reality was skewed, molded by the pressures of an immigrant mother, a trapped father, and a child unsure of her place in the world. To fully grasp my cognitive distortions and irrational beliefs, you'd need to delve into my story and my parents' stories.

Furthermore, you'd have to understand the ongoing realities for women in the Philippines to appreciate my unique perspective on politicized topics. My take on feminism, for instance, is colored by my experiences, viewing my rights as an American woman as a jackpot in the birth lottery.

Even with all the hardships, I never viewed myself as traumatized. How could I? I was saved, wasn't I? Swept into the sweet land of liberty, I felt lucky. If I ever faltered or failed, I believed it was on me because, after all, I had every opportunity to succeed.

The things that were beyond my control? I locked them away as if they never existed. The people who hurt me when I was younger, we moved away from them and so I pretended nothing ever happened. The fact that my father never uttered the words "I love you" or that his nickname for me meant "stupid" even though I made straight A's? I convinced myself that's just how fathers are, and I should be grateful to have one at all.

Perspective, in this sense, is both powerful and treacherous. So, how do we come to understand and wield this double-edged sword in a way that benefits us and those around us?

Shaping Reality: The Fluid Nature of Our Collective Understanding

Different environments shape your understanding of what's natural and normal, highlighting the fluid nature of reality. To dig deeper into this concept, let's look at a historical event that shook collective reality - the Copernican Revolution. Before the 16th century, people believed that the Earth was at the center of the universe. However, Copernicus' heliocentric model challenged this deeply ingrained reality, upending humanity's understanding of its place in the cosmos.

This example underscores how collective reality isn't static but evolves over time, shaped by scientific discoveries, cultural shifts, and societal changes. It highlights the dynamic nature of reality, constantly influenced by new insights and perspectives that challenge long-held beliefs. This process does not happen overnight and it can be volatile. As the saying goes, it gets worse before it gets better. Progress can be a challenging journey because it disrupts our familiar patterns of recognition, and many are hesitant to shift their beliefs.

By recognizing the ever-changing nature of collective reality, you open yourself up to a world of possibilities. You become more receptive to new ideas, more willing to question established norms, and more adaptable in the face of change. Embracing this fluidity allows you to grow as an individual and as a part of society, fostering a deeper appreciation for the interdependence of experiences and the ongoing evolution of 'The World We Know.'

Social Media's Influence on Reality

The malleability of reality has become increasingly evident in our digitally connected world. Within this interconnected environment, online personas are curated, crafting a digital reality that may not fully reflect actual experiences. These carefully curated identities and versions of life can significantly impact your perception of reality, leading you to compare your life with the idealized digital personas of others. The Netflix documentary "The Social Dilemma" powerfully argues that social media is eroding the shared sense of reality, which serves as the foundation of society.

This eye-opening documentary reveals the unintended harmful consequences of social media platforms that were originally designed to foster positive connections. It sheds light on how these platforms shape your beliefs and behaviors, ultimately leading to the erosion of trust and the rampant spread of misinformation. "The Social Dilemma" highlights the pivotal role of algorithms in creating filter bubbles and echo chambers, which restrict your exposure to diverse perspectives and fragmenting your understanding of reality. The consequences of this fragmented sense of reality are far-reaching, including social polarization and the manipulation of information.

In response to these complex issues, the documentary urges you to critically examine your relationship with social media. It calls for regulation and media literacy as crucial steps in addressing the challenges you face. "The Social Dilemma" prompts you to question the algorithms that govern your online experiences, actively seek out diverse perspectives, and cultivate a more balanced and informed digital environment.

By recognizing the impact of social media on the shared sense of reality, you can navigate the digital landscape more mindfully. It's essential to develop a critical awareness of the influences and biases inherent in your online interactions. Through this awareness, you can strive for a digital experience that promotes genuine connection, fosters a healthier understanding of reality, and strengthens the fabric of society.

Reality is far from being a fixed, universally agreed-upon concept. Shaped by countless factors – your background, culture, experiences, and even the era you live in – the world you know is, in essence, a personalized world, is a unique amalgamation of your subjective realities. You will explore how this malleable reality influences your perspectives, truths, and behaviors as you move forward. The journey may challenge some long-held notions, but remember, expanding your understanding of the world is the first step towards broadening your worldview.

Now, as we close this chapter, let's take a moment to reflect on what we've learned and consider how we can incorporate these insights into our daily lives.

Chapter 1 Action Items

Let's take further action with these concepts to understand how we define our reality.

* **Reflect** on how your perception of reality may have been shaped by your experiences and influences.

Introspection and open-minded exploration brings us closer to a richer, more nuanced understanding of our realities.

CHAPTER 2

The Art of Changing Your Mind

Exposure Sparks Transformation

A few years before my challenging period of self-discovery, I had the privilege of meeting Dandapani, a Hindu priest, speaker, and entrepreneur. Our encounter took place in a light and bright conference hall, nestled by a serene lake, its waters mirroring the clear blue of a perfectly sunny day. The impeccable green of the grass seemed to stretch endlessly, adding to the tranquility of the setting.

Dandapani stood out, not just for his words, but for his presence. He wore a natural-colored priest robe paired with flowing white pants, and around his neck hung Rudraksha meditation beads. His head, either shaved or naturally bald, carried three white lines of paint across the forehead, above a red dot situated between his eyebrows. His demeanor was calm, yet there was an infectious joy about him. It was evident not just in his speech, but in the way he took the time after his talk, lingering, valuing our time and presence. The gentle scent of eucalyptus wafted in the air, a calming backdrop provided by candles handed out as gifts by our hosts.

His words, emphasizing the immutability of the past, might also resonate with you. At the time, I only heard his words when he said, "The past cannot be changed, forgotten, or erased; it can only be accepted." While I believed him, I didn't fully feel the weight of his message then.

It wasn't that his words lacked impact; they lingered and resonated long after. Yet, immediate transformation eluded me. True self-transformation required my effort to release my past, heightened my awareness, and mastered my mind.

At times, I found myself echoing the actions of change, while in other moments, doubt crept in. 'Why isn't change easier? Why can't I just snap and transform?' But every challenge reminded me that growth often feels like taking two steps forward and one step back.

As I reflect on that time, I know now that I did not realize how many steps backward I had taken due to past trauma. It tinted my perceptions and my world views in a way that I could not even recognize for myself. Yet I kept taking small steps forward, mimicking the leader I wanted to become.

As a leader, perhaps you can appreciate that exposure and time with other luminaries like Dandapani are invaluable. At the time, I hadn't fully realized the depth of his wisdom. But when it eventually dawned on me, it was like the first ray of sunshine after a long storm — a profound sense of gratitude, tinged with the wish that I had understood it sooner.

My journey of self-discovery and healing, intertwined with the themes I'm exploring in this book, wasn't without its hurdles. These weren't ordinary bumps in the road but profound moments of reckoning that tested my resolve and reshaped my understanding of myself.

Your personal journey, like everyone's, is a unique tapestry woven from experiences, challenges, and insights. It's not just about recounting what you've been through, but truly understanding these moments within a wider context. As you confront fear or face heart-pounding memories, remember that these emotions, while deeply personal, are also valid and universally human.

Through vulnerability and resilience, you'll come to see that it's not just about overcoming challenges, but understanding their origins, their impact, and how they influence your identity. It's also about opening yourself up to the journey of the person sitting across from you. In life, much like in business, market timing, awareness, and acceptance are pivotal. Equally significant are the factors influencing your personal growth. You have the power to rediscover yourself and harness the transformative potential that lies within.

As I share pieces of my story and my findings from various studies, consider them mirrors. They're designed to reflect parts of your journey, to illuminate pathways for introspection — helping you navigate the intricate tapestry of your beliefs and experiences.

"We don't see things as they are;
we see them as we are."

ANAÏS NIN

The Power of Social Environments

I'm reminded of a case study from the mid-20th century that still resonates with me today. In 1954, psychologists Muzafer Sherif and his wife, Carolyn Wood Sherif, embarked on a unique exploration of human nature that came to be known as the 'Robbers Cave Experiment.' Their stage for this project was a humble summer camp filled with unsuspecting 11- and 12-year-old boys.

At first glance, these boys were strikingly similar, their lives marked by comparable backgrounds and experiences. However, when the Sherifs divided the boys into two separate teams, a transformation occurred that was as fascinating as it was alarming. Within each group, a distinct sense of identity began to crystallize, carving out an invisible boundary that screamed "us–versus–them."

I can't help but picture the scene: the once-unified group of boys now divided, their shared camaraderie fragmented into an escalating dance of conflict and hostility. It's the real life version of the movie 'Lord of the Flies.' Propelled by a fierce loyalty to their group and an equally strong urge to guard their newfound identities, the boys engaged in competitions and exhibited negative behaviors against the other team.

The 'Robbers Cave Experiment,' in its stark simplicity, serves as a powerful mirror reflecting how swiftly and effortlessly our immediate social environment can sculpt our perceptions and realities. It makes me wonder about the boys and their individual or collective experiences and how an arbitrary line in the sand had the power to create such a formidable sense of group identity, enough to fuel fires of conflict among friends.

This case study is one that underscores the potent sway of social dynamics and their capacity to mold our reality. It's a sobering reminder of how vital it is to nurture inclusivity in

our environments, to dissolve those invisible boundaries before they harden into walls. In fact, as the boys in the 'Robbers Cave Experiment' discovered, our realities are more malleable than we often realize.

From Teammate to Opponent

There's another narrative from the acclaimed television series "Ted Lasso" that you may relate to if you played team sports or if you're an avid sports fan. The narrative is an exploration of competition's impact on team dynamics that resonates far beyond the confines of a football field.

Even if you're unfamiliar with the series, the narrative of one particular episode, "International Break," serves as an illuminating study in human behavior.

In this episode, we witness several Richmond football team players, including the effervescent Dani Rojas, stepping into new roles as they represent their respective countries. Known for his infectious positivity and unwavering support for his team, Dani's transformation is a sight to behold. As he dons the colors of Mexico in the international tournament, I notice a marked shift in his demeanor. His usually bright presence takes on a darker, more intimidating hue—a reflection, perhaps, of the combative mindset that comes with being an adversary.

In a moment that shocks me and, I'm sure, many viewers, Dani goes so far as to break the nose of his Richmond teammate, Van Damme, during the heated match between Canada and Mexico. The fierce competition, Dani's binding loyalty to his national team, it all seems to push Dani into a space where his usual jovial self is lost.

Then, the International Break concludes, and we witness a return to normalcy. The players retreat from their national roles, resuming their familiar positions as teammates. Dani, once again, embodies the gentle, kind, and cheerful person we know. However, there's a lingering moment that stays

with me: he does not immediately apologize to Van Damme for the injury inflicted during their stint as rivals.

This narrative from "Ted Lasso" offers a compelling reminder of the complex dance between camaraderie and rivalry that sporting events often incite. It underscores how significantly representing one's country can alter an athlete's mindset and behavior, highlighting the intricate dynamics of team relationships and the delicate balance between personal identity, loyalty, and shared success.

As I contemplate these ideas, I can't help but ask: What does it take to change our minds? How do our minds shift in different environments? How do our perceptions seep into our behaviors and attitudes?

As we embark on this exploration together, let's remember that we're delving not only into the objective world but also into our intricate web of perceptions.

Chapter 2 Action Items

Practicing self awareness of how these concepts impact our views is the first step to building bridges of understanding. Here are some action items that you can put into practice.

* **Explore** how team competitions and social constructs have influenced your behaviors and your views of others.

* **Challenge your assumptions** by seeking out alternative sources of information and exposing yourself to diverse viewpoints.

CHAPTER 3

The Power of Perspective

Continuing your journey through 'The World We Know,' we move from understanding the malleability of reality to exploring the profound impact of our point of view. As simple as it sounds, your perspective holds the power to shape your interactions, experiences, and, ultimately, your version of reality.

Perceiving the Unseen

The ancient parable of the six blind men and the elephant provides an excellent starting point to reflect on the power of perspective.

In this story, a group of blind men who have never encountered an elephant before makes a remarkable discovery. As they explore the magnificent creature with their hands, each blind man touches a different part of the elephant and forms a unique impression based on their limited perspective.

The man who feels the trunk, in awe of its snakelike nature, proclaims the elephant to be a creature of sleekness and grace. The one who encounters the leg, sturdy and grounded, insists the elephant is reminiscent of a massive tree. Another, grasping the tail, envisions a creature swaying like a broom. Each blind man fervently defends their interpretation, convinced that their truth is the only truth.

This compelling tale serves as a powerful metaphor for the limitations of your individual perspective and the intricate nature of reality itself. As you reflect upon this story, question the nature of truth and how your own experiences shape your understanding of 'The World We Know.'

The story of the blind men and the elephant, while simple, carries profound implications for your interactions with others. It invites you to embrace humility and curiosity, recognizing that your own perspectives are just fragments of a greater whole.

As you navigate the labyrinth of perception, remember the tale of the blind men and the enigmatic elephant. This story underscores the importance of embracing multiple perspectives and acknowledging that the complete truth often lies beyond your individual grasp. By embracing the richness of collective wisdom, you inch closer to unraveling the mysteries of 'The World We Know' and understanding the complex realities that surround you. Together, we explore these intricacies and complexities, charting the course through this fascinating exploration of reality.

Different Workplace Perspectives and Experiences

Parables can often help us relate to real-world scenarios. Take, for instance, the story of Anna and John, two employees in the same office. They both report to a stern and no-nonsense boss. Anna sees her boss as a tyrant, and she is anxious and stressed throughout her workday. In contrast, John views the same boss as a strict but fair individual and appreciates the discipline in his work environment. The boss remains the same, but Anna and John's differing perspectives shape their distinct work experiences.

As leaders, we may not necessarily change how we lead based on individual preferences. It does mean that we may get along with some team members better than others. I have witnessed this affecting hiring decisions in an effort to hire applicants who are more like us so that we have what

we perceive to be a more harmonious work environment. Despite the studies that show diverse teams lead to greater innovation and success. For this reason, Anna may never speak up for how hard her work environment is for her. Additionally, Anna may not recognize that her perspective is not solely based on her interactions with her boss. It's a tight rope in management and leadership. However, culture experts are recognizing that learning about ourselves is as important as learning about our team and how we can work together. With the right training, Anna, John and their boss can become the best team.

The Multifaceted Reality

As you consider this scenario, keep in mind its implications for team dynamics and culture. Remember that more perspectives exist than just those of Anna and John. If you were a leader in this workplace, you would need to go beyond finding surface-level solutions to conflicts arising from two differing perspectives. Instead, you would step into the shoes of everyone involved, exploring their unique experiences. As a leader, it is crucial to transcend the role of a problem-solver and embrace the role of an empathetic listener.

By considering the perspectives of Anna, John, their boss, and others connected to this story, you open yourself up to a deeper understanding of the impact of your actions and behaviors on those around you. Recognizing that your responses and behaviors are influenced by your own awareness and understanding, you can cultivate empathy, bridge gaps, and foster a more inclusive and harmonious workplace culture.

As organizational psychologists have found, people in the workplace and in life can have starkly different reactions to the same situations due to their unique perspectives. These perspectives are influenced by personality, past experiences, values, and even a person's current mood.

Conflicting Perspectives on a Global Scale

Next, consider a significant historical event through various lenses. As an extreme example, the dropping of atomic bombs on Hiroshima and Nagasaki during WWII can be seen from one perspective as a horrifying act causing immense loss of life. Yet, from another perspective, it can also be viewed as a necessary evil that ended the war. The facts of the event itself are the same, but perspectives vary, demonstrating how an individual's viewpoint can affect

their interpretation of the same event. In the next chapter, we provide examples of the duality of truth which might provide some comfort for those grappling with extreme and horrific scenarios such as this.

Cultural Relativism

The common practice of interpreting experiences differently extends beyond individuals and events to encompass entire societies and cultures. What's considered polite in one culture might be seen as rude in another. For instance, maintaining eye contact, which signifies honesty and confidence in many Western cultures, is often considered disrespectful in several East Asian cultures.

This is referred to as cultural relativism. This is the idea that cultural beliefs, values, and practices should be understood and evaluated within their own cultural context. This means that there are no universal standards to judge or compare different societies. Instead, each society should be respected and understood on its own terms, without imposing one's own cultural values on others.

Cultural relativism recognizes the diversity of the human experience and encourages an open-minded and non-judgmental attitude toward cultural differences. It emphasizes the importance of understanding and appreciating different perspectives and moral systems found in various parts of the world. By embracing cultural relativism, you begin to promote mutual respect and foster intercultural understanding.

The Influence of Others' Perspectives on Our Behaviors and Responses

With this foundation in mind, let's now transition to another vital aspect: the impact of other people's perspectives on our behaviors and responses. While you have explored how your own perspectives and experiences shape your understanding, it is equally important to consider how the perspectives of others can influence your actions and outcomes.

In an enlightening study, psychologist Dr. Robert Rosenthal shed light on the intriguing aspect of influence, revealing that teachers' expectations of their students had a significant effect on their performance. The teachers' perspectives not only influenced their personal interactions with the students but also impacted the students' behavior and academic achievement. This powerful influence is called the Pygmalion Effect.[1]

In upcoming sections, we will delve deeper into the intricate nature of your worldview, examining how those in positions of power or in the public eye can shape your perspective, and in turn, influence your behaviors and responses. As you navigate 'The World We Know,' it's crucial to recognize the profound impact that the beliefs and expectations of others can have on your life.

Lady Bird Johnson beautifully encapsulated this idea when she commented on our beliefs about children.

*"Children are apt to live up to
what you believe of them."*

LADY BIRD JOHNSON

These words highlight the significant role that the beliefs and perspectives of others play in shaping your behaviors and shaping your potential for growth and success.

Take my story, for example. My mother, an immigrant from the Philippines had beliefs that certainly influenced my belief system and shaped my behaviors. Alternatively, my father had beliefs that I defied and fought against in my attempts to prove that I was better than he believed. Those beliefs, while very different from my mother's, still had a profound impact on my behavior. Not only did I need to prove myself to him, since I felt I never measured up, even after his death I held on to my need to feel worthy. It was in many cases my driving motivation. But worthy of what? I no longer knew. That has been a part of my exploration as I write these pages.

Remember that your perspectives are powerful and so are the perspectives of those around you. They shape your understanding, color your experiences, and influence your responses. It impacts our interactions, our relationships and our dissatisfaction or happiness. Recognizing this power is critical as you attempt to broaden your perspectives and understand the myriad of realities that constitute 'The World We Know.' The next chapter will delve into the intriguing duality of truth, another concept that I found pivotal to my healing.

Chapter 3 Action Items

The power of perspective can change the way we interact with one another. Here are a few action items to continue working on the concepts in this chapter:

* **Engage in perspective-taking exercises**, such as writing from the point of view of someone with opposing beliefs.

* **Seek out diverse sources of information** including books, articles, podcasts, and documentaries, to broaden your understanding of different perspectives.

* **Practice awareness** of how your perspectives influence others. Also, recognize your feelings of discomfort and seek to understand the narratives that create these reactions. Surround yourself with people who positively influence your awareness and perspectives.

CHAPTER 4

Embracing the Duality of Truth

Having journeyed through the malleability of reality and unpacked the power of perspective, we now arrive at a seemingly paradoxical concept: the duality of truth. While truth is often considered singular and absolute, it is essential to recognize that different truths can coexist.

Honesty is something that I value greatly. Many companies post this on their walls and t-shirts as an important core value. However, honesty is rooted in truth, and people can hold different, but still very valid truths. From personal conflicts to significant historical events, the duality of truth becomes evident when examining how different perspectives shape your understanding of reality.

One example stemming from corporate America is the story of Andy Fastow, the former CFO of Enron. A few years ago, I had the opportunity to hear Andy speak and share his side of the story. He does not defend his actions or try to prove innocence.

Andy was convicted and took the fall for Enron. However, the facts do reveal that there are many different truths throughout this story. For one, Andy was winning award after award for his skills as the CFO of Enron. The way he managed the finances were celebrated and praised by financial leaders. Until, they weren't. The facts did not change, but the widely accepted views on those practices shifted. What was right and wrong came into question.

He shares that he did everything by the book, and everything was signed off and approved. However, he knows in his heart what is right and wrong. He knows that what they did as a corporation and his role in that was wrong. What's surprising is the same scenarios that led to success also led to failure.

A Family Dispute: Perspectives in Conflict

Let's explore a more personal scenario. Picture a typical family dispute. A mother scolds her son for coming home late without informing her. In response, the son asserts that he is old enough to care for himself. In this scenario, both the mother and the son hold their own truths. The mother, driven by concern for her son's safety, regards her scolding as necessary. Meanwhile, the son, seeking independence, sees it as an imposition on his freedom.

These contrasting truths exist simultaneously, highlighting the concept of duality in personal relationships. This example shows how individuals, influenced by their unique experiences and perspectives, can interpret and react to the same situation differently. It serves as a reminder that acknowledging and navigating this duality of truth is key to promoting mutual understanding and harmony in our interactions.

The Influence of Perspectives on Belief and Morality

In understanding the duality of truth, let's first acknowledge that your beliefs and moral values are not solely based on reason.

Your understanding of the world and what is truthful, derived from a myriad of factors — cultural background, personal experiences, education, and more — gives rise to your unique perspective.

This perspective serves as the lens through which you view the world and significantly shapes your belief systems and moral judgments. Moral sense philosophers argue that emotions and feelings, deeply influenced by your worldview, play a crucial role in shaping your moral compass.

Therefore, in the upcoming exploration of how emotions influence your worldview, you'll uncover how perspectives mold your beliefs and morality. Acknowledging and understanding this influence allows you to better navigate the complexities of 'The World We Know' and appreciate the diversity of moral codes and belief systems that exist.

A Tapestry of Multiple Realities in Historical Narratives

Keeping this concept in mind, consider the narrative of colonization as an example of the duality of truth in historical events. From the colonizers' viewpoint, their actions were seen as a means of civilizing lands and peoples they perceived as 'savage.' On the other hand, the colonized experienced these same actions as subjugation, exploitation, and a loss of cultural identity. These contrasting viewpoints coexist, illustrating the complex and multidimensional nature of historical events and the writing and documentation of history. Interestingly, the morality of the colonizers' actions is perceived differently depending on one's perspective, further highlighting the impact of one's worldview on their understanding of truth and morality.

This example underscores that 'The World We Know' isn't static. As noted before in the example of the Copernican Revolution, it evolves over time, influenced by scientific discoveries, cultural shifts, and societal changes. This reveals the dynamic nature of reality, constantly shaped by new insights and perspectives challenging long-held beliefs. You may find yourself resisting these discoveries. For example, I was very reluctant to accept Pluto's planetary demotion because I was always taught that our solar system has nine planets. More controversial than the number of planets are the discussions about sex at birth and gender and how that is changing our approach to policies and societal norms.

When I reflect on the impact of these societal beliefs and new discoveries on my reality and behaviors, I realize that demoting Pluto does not affect me. Understanding and appreciating someone's gender impacts my ability to live out my values as a respectful, inclusive person. And so regardless of the worldviews when I was raised, I need to be aware of current worldviews and decide how I want to show up in the world. Do I allow myself to be hindered by my existing beliefs? I've already answered that question for myself on this and many other controversial topics that are prolific in early 21st-century news, social media, entertainment, and politics.

I discussed a similar contentious issue with a friend. "I don't judge, and honestly, I don't care much about it," they stated calmly. "I'm just tired of the constant noise surrounding this topic because it doesn't impact my life," they continued.

I contemplated their perspective and posed a question, "If you don't care, does it really matter to you if policies related to this issue change?" I inquired.

My friend responded animatedly, "It's a bit more complex than that because I believe politicians often fail to consider the full spectrum of experiences and nuances. What we hear are the extreme, polarized viewpoints, and matters are presented as either right or wrong. The problem is that policies should serve everyone, not just the most vocal voices. They can't be crafted solely to appease the loudest factions, as that disregards the broader impact on those who aren't as outspoken."

Is there a right or wrong answer? I don't know.

> *"There is nothing either good or bad,*
> *but thinking makes it so."*

> WILLIAM SHAKESPEARE

I recognize that I need to think through my beliefs and behaviors. I also accept that it's okay to change my mind when I have more information.

As someone who strongly believes in our freedoms, such politicized and extreme topics remind me of a quote from Noam Chomsky.

> *"If you're really in favor of free speech,*
> *then you're in favor of freedom of speech*
> *for precisely the views you despise."*

> NOAM CHOMSKY

When faced with uncomfortable topics, I challenge you to understand your aversion and to wrestle with your understanding.

Recognizing the existence of multiple truths can be an enlightening tool when examining history. This realization allows you to see past the single narrative often presented in textbooks and invites you to delve into the complexities and nuances of historical events. Understanding that the colonizer and the colonized might have entirely different perspectives on the same events prompts deeper reflection on the stories we are told and those we tell ourselves.

Being aware that multiple truths can exist in historical narratives empowers you to examine history and history in the making with a more critical eye, seeking out different perspectives and questioning the singular narrative. You begin to appreciate the complexity of historical events and understand the shaping forces behind our collective memory. This consciousness, in turn, helps you recognize that truths, much like the pages of history, can be more layered and multifaceted than they first appear.

Finding Truth in Physics: The Wave-Particle Duality

In physics, there is an intriguing concept known as wave-particle duality. This principle posits that light can display both wave-like and particle-like properties, contingent on how you observe or measure it.

Scientists studying light have noticed its chameleon-like nature: under some experimental conditions, it behaves like a wave, exhibiting properties such as interference and diffraction. However, under other circumstances, it reveals its particle side, interacting with matter as discrete particles known as photons. Both views of light's character—wave and particle—are equally valid, and integral to our comprehensive understanding of its nature.

This duality within light's nature defies intuition, suggesting that light can concurrently exist as both a wave and a particle. This quantum mechanical phenomenon challenges traditional notions of light, and it serves as a potent reminder: truth can present itself in multiple, context-dependent facets, even within the precise realm of scientific research.

Just as light can exist in different forms depending on the context, your perception of truth is shaped by your experiences, perspectives, and observations. This understanding of reality can vary based on the lens through which you view it, underlining the significance of wave-particle duality in both the physical and metaphorical sense. This concept serves as a compelling invitation to embrace the notion that truth isn't fixed or singular, but fluid and context-dependent.

The duality of light is pretty fascinating. It encourages recognition and appreciation for the coexistence of multiple truths, even if they seem to contradict each other. If you can really embrace this concept, it opens up a lot of doors. You become better at understanding other people's points of view, and that can make your interactions with others richer and more respectful. Ultimately, it helps you realize that the truths shaping your reality can look different depending on where you're standing.

A Tale of Two Perspectives: The City Experience

Returning to a more everyday context, let's immerse ourselves in a day in New York City. Picture Lara and Lynn, two city dwellers experiencing the city's vibrant pulse. Lara, a seasoned New Yorker, cherishes the city's energy. To her, skyscrapers are marvels of architecture, the markets are bustling centers of diversity, and the city itself is a broad stage of opportunity.

Meanwhile, Lynn, fresh from a small town and new to city life, perceives a different truth. The city's constant hum feels more overwhelming than lively. The towering buildings appear intimidating, and the persistent noise

leaves her disoriented. The city feels impersonal and lacks the cozy charm of her hometown.

In this cityscape, Lara and Lynn each harbor their own truths. Their personal experiences and viewpoints color their perceptions, a vivid example of the duality of truth. Lara's reality celebrates the city's energy and potential, while Lynn's centers on its overwhelming nature and the impact on her comfort level.

Yet, this doesn't mean Lynn is destined to feel perpetually overwhelmed. By stepping outside her comfort zone—perhaps by attending a local community event or discovering a quiet café in her neighborhood—she might find elements of the city that are comforting and familiar, gradually reshaping her view.

The essence of New York City remains unchanged, but Lara and Lynn's experiences are remarkably different. This stark difference shows how our individual truths, although contrasting, are valid and based on our genuine experiences.

Embracing this understanding can enhance your interactions with others, nurture empathy, and spark curiosity about alternative perspectives. Additionally, it can encourage you to venture outside your comfort zones, leading to broader perspectives and richer life experiences.

Engaging a Mediator: Resolving Conflicts through Perspective

Now, let's shift gears and consider a less grandiose but equally relatable example. Imagine two neighbors entangled in a heated dispute over a tree that sits right on their property line. It might sound trivial, but these sorts of disputes can get quite serious. Especially in places like the state of Illinois, where property laws indicate that even if most of a tree resides on one person's property, they can't do much without the other property owner's consent.

In this story, both neighbors have different ideas about who owns the tree and how to manage it. Things get so tense that they have to bring in a mediator to help find some common ground. And here's where the magic happens: the mediator helps each neighbor see the situation from the other person's perspective, which eventually leads them to a resolution they can both live with.

This doesn't mean we're denying that there are factual and legal aspects to consider. There's a tree, a property line, and specific laws in Illinois that affect the outcome. Those are objective facts. But what the mediator was able to do was to bring each neighbor's subjective truth into the discussion, shaping a fuller understanding of the situation and eventually leading to an amicable resolution.

So, what does this mean for you? Well, it's about considering how different perspectives can illuminate a situation, even when objective facts are involved. It's about understanding that solutions often lie in the space where different truths overlap. And most importantly, it's a reminder that stepping into someone else's shoes and viewing the world through their lens can often be the key to unlocking conflict and fostering understanding.

While I have remained somewhat black and white in my descriptions, naming this chapter the duality of truth, and providing examples of one perspective against an opposing perspective, I know and hope you have also uncovered as you ponder these scenarios that there is an array of colored lenses that tint reality and shape our truths.

As you will see in the next chapter, your version of reality and memory of a specific scenario may be imperfect, influenced, or broken. Despite that, it does not negate real events or the facts of those events. Only that your version of a story may not be the same as another person who has experienced the same incident. That inconsistency does not discount what is real in your mind, but it does warrant exploration towards understanding.

Chapter 4 Action Items

To navigate the duality of truth effectively and promote a deeper understanding, consider the following action items:

* **Foster cognitive flexibility**: Intentionally explore multiple perspectives on a given topic before forming your own opinion. This practice enhances your ability to grasp the complexity of truth.

* **Engage in respectful debates and discussions**: Seek out opportunities to engage in conversations with others who hold opposing viewpoints. By understanding their perspectives, you can challenge your own beliefs and broaden your understanding.

* **Explore diverse narratives**: Read books or articles that offer different perspectives on historical events or social issues. By exposing yourself to a range of viewpoints, you can gain a deeper appreciation for the multifaceted nature of truth and enhance your ability to engage in informed discussions.

* **Practice intellectual humility**: Recognize the limitations of your own knowledge and remain open to the

possibility of learning from others. Embracing intellectual humility allows you to approach discussions and disagreements with an open mind, fostering a spirit of curiosity and continuous learning.

Remember, the exploration of truth is an ongoing process. Reflect on what you've learned and how it can inform your understanding of the world. Isn't it fascinating how your beliefs shape your reality? As you move into the next chapter, you're going to lean into the intriguing dance between perception and cognition, revealing more insights that can help you navigate your own reality more effectively.

CHAPTER 5

Belief As Truth

A Complex Tapestry

As you traverse 'The World We Know,' you encounter an intriguing crossroads where belief intersects with the truth. In your journey, you'll find that these constructs are closely interwoven, with beliefs often transforming into personal truths, shaping your attitudes, actions, and interpretations of the world.

The Influence of Belief and Confirmation Bias

How does this interplay between belief and truth surface in your everyday life? Often, it takes the form of confirmation bias, a psychological phenomenon where you are naturally inclined to seek, interpret, and remember information that aligns with your pre-existing beliefs. At the same time, you may unintentionally dismiss or overlook information that contradicts your worldview.

It's like what philosopher and psychologist William James once observed:

"Belief creates the actual fact."

WILLIAM JAMES

An example that illustrates this powerfully is the ongoing debate on climate change. Even with substantial scientific evidence supporting its reality, some individuals vehemently deny its existence. Political ideologies or economic interests may sway these skeptics, leading them to selectively engage with data that bolster their stance, effectively transforming belief into personal truth.

The Human Brain: A Fortress of Beliefs

Did you know that your brain naturally strives to maintain consistency in your belief system? Often, it finds it easier to discard conflicting information than to re-evaluate your long-held beliefs. If you are familiar with Albert Ellis and his Cognitive Behavioral Therapy (CBT), you might recognize this challenging aspect of the way our mind works. Learning and acknowledging our irrational beliefs might seem simple, but changing these beliefs is often far from easy. In fact, it can sometimes feel uncomfortably difficult. During my journey I have found that most of the barriers to changing my mind and my behaviors were not external, but internal – conflicts with my own beliefs and narratives.

Awareness and a willingness to change marks the first step in modifying our beliefs, and thus our responses and behaviors, but it's common to encounter unconscious resistance. Your brain, over time, has crafted neural pathways akin to rivers carving their course through the Earth. These pathways shape your understanding and habitual responses. Over time, your repeated thoughts and behaviors create entrenched pathways in your brain that become more automatic. To alter or divert these automated pathways demands conscious effort and time to establish new thinking patterns and behaviors.

Your beliefs can influence your perception of truth, molding both individual and collective narratives. Let's explore a more radical side of beliefs: the infamous 'Roswell Incident' of 1947. When a U.S. military balloon crashed near Roswell, New Mexico, the military asserted it was a mere weather balloon. Yet, some people chose to believe it was the remains of an extraterrestrial spacecraft despite a lack of tangible evidence.

Over time, this belief morphed into a 'truth' for some, leading to countless conspiracy theories and popularizing ideas of UFOs and alien cover-ups.

The power of belief is formidable, isn't it? Let's explore this further in the next section.

The Placebo and Nocebo Effect

Have you ever considered how your beliefs can directly influence your physical health? Let's look at the medical field, where the strength of belief introduces intriguing phenomena like the placebo and nocebo effects. A placebo, despite having no actual therapeutic properties, can result in improvements in your condition if you wholeheartedly believe it's a genuine cure. On the other hand, the nocebo effect reflects the flip side of this coin, where your symptoms can worsen in response to negative expectations. These instances powerfully illustrate the capacity of our minds, showcasing how belief, whether it is positive or negative, can bring about tangible physical outcomes.

This influence and effect is further seen in health practices that emphasize the mind-body connection, the compelling link between your thoughts, attitudes, behaviors, and overall physical health. This highlights how your emotions and your mental state can significantly impact your well-being and even longevity. Central to the principles of holistic medicine, this connection focuses on treating you as a whole person, not just addressing symptoms. Today, healthcare professionals across the board acknowledge the importance of a more comprehensive approach that harmoniously integrates mind, body, and spirit for optimal care.

Beliefs: Tinted Lenses of Perception

Consider your beliefs as the unique lens through which you view the world, a lens crafted and colored by your individual experiences. These lenses aren't merely observational tools. They actively shape your reality, illuminating certain aspects while gently shading and tinting others to create a personalized picture of the world around you.

Just like the variety of lenses in a camera bag, each one of us carries our unique perspective. These lenses aren't inherently right or wrong, better or worse; they're simply different, offering us an intimate and individual way of interacting with the world.

However, being aware that these lenses can occasionally distort, amplify or obscure our view can be powerful. It's not about discarding our existing lenses, but rather understanding their nature, acknowledging their influence, and learning how to adjust our focus when needed.

Understanding this encourages a state of openness and curiosity. It can inspire us to occasionally swap lenses, see the world from different angles, and gain a broader understanding of the complexities around us.

This approach doesn't belittle the value of your current beliefs. Instead, it honors them while gently promoting openness to enrich them further. It fosters a space where 'my truth' and 'your truth' can coexist, respecting the rich diversity of human experiences. This mutual respect and understanding is a crucial stepping stone to navigating the complexities of human interactions and beliefs.

Having covered the influence of belief on our perception of truth, you're now prepared to delve into the intriguing realm of cognitive dissonance in the next section.

A Profound Cognitive Dissonance

Understanding the intricate dance between belief and truth, you might be asking yourself: What happens when sincere truth is met with disbelief? How does this dissonance affect our perception of reality and, in turn, our mental well-being?

When we face skepticism towards our truths, it can trigger internal conflicts that resonate within us, leading to serious emotional turmoil. As we explore this concept further, I would like to invite you into my personal journey. I hope it helps illuminate the power of belief, its implications on our mental health, and the arduous yet liberating path of overcoming self-limiting beliefs.

Liberation from Self-Limiting Beliefs

It's said that overcoming limiting beliefs is a crucial step toward mental liberation. This journey is far from easy—it often involves confronting past traumas and rewriting deeply ingrained narratives. However, it's through these struggles that we can achieve transformative growth and build greater resilience against future challenges.

On my path of self-discovery and healing, I once received a rather striking label from a therapist. He noted that I am a "high-functioning dysfunctional person." I wore this label with a bit of pride. This characterization echoed within me; it captured the paradox of my existence. On the outside, I was successfully navigating the world. Yet, inwardly, I was a cauldron of unchecked emotions - anxiety, stress, fear, shame, frustration - all simmering and ready to boil over at the slightest provocation.

My journey toward healing truly began when I found myself spiraling out of control. As painful as this crisis was, it served as the catalyst for my path to recovery. Before I could rebuild, however, I had to deconstruct my inner world—a process I liken to a caterpillar entering the chrysalis stage: a complete disintegration before the subsequent transformation.

The root of my struggle was an insidious belief: "I am not important enough to be believed." The seeds of this belief were planted in my childhood, when, at the age of five, I found myself grappling with fear and confusion. Unraveling the persistent grip of this belief on my adult life required the emotionally draining task of revisiting fragments of past traumas.

The process was a stark reminder that success in the external world doesn't safeguard against internal struggles. As a successful business owner, I had constructed an armor of achievement. Yet, it did nothing to shield me from my inner turmoil. Instead, it created a rift between my public persona and my private reality, landing me in a cycle of self-loathing. I was eager for rapid change but confronted with the reality of slow and painstaking progress.

During these dark times, a strong support network proved to be my lifeline. Even though I was embedded in this supportive cocoon, I quickly realized that transforming my belief system wouldn't be an overnight process. Despite my intellectual understanding and intense desire for change, I felt trapped in the dichotomy of my realities. The breakthrough came when I finally confronted this dissonance head-on and decided to reconcile the differences.

My pivotal moment occurred when I revisited the memory of my five-year- old self, finally understanding that my limited vocabulary at that tender age was incapable of expressing the magnitude of my distress. At that age, I knew that God was good and the Devil was evil. When I shared that "the Devil comes for me," it was not a case of intentional dismissal from others; they simply couldn't understand what I was trying to share and I did not have the words for what was happening to me. And without that understanding, they couldn't grasp the depth of my pain. This revelation brought a sense of closure and kindled a strength within me, allowing me to start releasing the self-limiting belief that held me captive for so long.

Today, even though encountering situations of disbelief or distrust remains a challenge, they no longer have the power to debilitate me. I have a voice and I have the ability to choose how I react and respond to these situations.

I have gradually reshaped my perspective, embracing and accepting the idea that the understanding of others may be fallible. Also, that my truth may be different that theirs, despite how real it is for me. In doing so, I've fostered a greater sense of resilience.

It's an ongoing endeavor, this journey of breaking free from my past, but it's one that I endure with amazing support, newfound courage, and relentless determination.

The Role of Validation

The relationship between truth and belief is not always clear; it twists and turns as it pleases like a murky, organic river. Think about this journey we've taken exploring belief systems. Have you considered the importance of external validation? Imagine someone questions or outright denies your truth. You'd likely feel your self-esteem take a hit. This underscores the key role of empathy and support in both our personal stories and the narratives we share as a community. Without validation, it's easy to feel alone and start doubting ourselves, which can lead to mental health struggles.

What happens when someone dismisses your heartfelt truth? When do the shared realities you rely on begin to crumble under the weight of disbelief? Let's consider these questions: How do your belief systems and shared truths interact? What role do trust and mutual understanding play in your communities?

As you continue to explore these complex themes, keep these questions in mind and refer back to the action items provided at the end of each chapter. By making an effort to understand someone else's beliefs and the truth of their reality, you may start to empathize with the disbelief others may feel. This can be the first step in bridging the gap between differing viewpoints.

Navigating Disbelief and Fluid Realities for Mental Well-being

The journey toward mental well-being in the face of disbelief can be arduous. It is a harrowing experience when personal truths are met with dismissive attitudes or disbelief, leading to feelings of self-doubt, hopelessness, and a deep sense of invalidation. Some can experience a decline in their mental health due to this. Therefore, it's essential for leaders, regardless of whether you are in a business, community, social, or familial setting, to foster safe environments that help encourage open-mindedness, constructive conversation, and trust.

Creating conditions that ensure individuals feel heard and supported is crucial in spaces where an exchange of ideas takes place such as workplaces, educational institutions, or any community-based discussions. Beyond these settings where such a structure is necessary to achieve goals successfully, finding or co-creating these spaces with others invites safety and allows for shared realities.

We live in a world where realities are malleable, perspectives can be influenced, and truths can be dualistic or even multifaceted in nature. In this world, disbelief or lack of trust can lead to a diminished sense of self and fracture our shared understanding.

It is always important to engage in constructive dialogues about beliefs, truths, and their impacts on our physical and mental well-being. And now, more than ever, we need to evaluate and better understand the factors that shape our reality and recognize that those factors are different for each person that sits next to us. Conflict, disagreements and more importantly, outright disbelief and denial of another person's reality can cause unintentional harm.

The resulting behaviors from stress, anxiety, burnout, mental disorders, and a reduced sense of self acceptance or self love can be damaging to ourselves and others.

Are you ready to take action on these concepts? Perhaps you need more time to consider all of the factors that are influencing your belief systems and your perspectives.

Chapter 5 Action Items

* **Reflect on the beliefs you hold as "truth"** and critically examine the evidence and reasoning behind them.

* **Engage in constructive conversations** with individuals who hold different beliefs and seek to understand their perspectives.

* **Regularly expose yourself to diverse sources** of information to challenge confirmation bias and broaden your understanding of complex issues. Converse with individuals who hold different beliefs and seek to understand their perspectives.

* **Practice being open** to revisiting your long-held beliefs when presented with new evidence or compelling arguments for deeper understanding.

Exploring the intricate dance between belief and truth offers insights into the workings of your mind and how you interact with yourself and with others. By recognizing the influence of these dynamics, a conscious approach becomes possible, empowering you to navigate disagreements with empathy and create environments of mutual understanding.

CHAPTER 6

Worldview Through Society's Prism

Within the intricate tapestry of society, you are woven into a complex web of social structures that profoundly influence your perspectives and shape your worldview.

Like a prism, society acts as a powerful refractor of realities, splintering them into a kaleidoscope of colors that represent cultural norms, shared beliefs, and societal values. These collective influences sculpt your perceptions, laying the groundwork for how you interpret and engage with your surroundings.

We are all immensely connected, and yet, uniquely separate and distinct. This chapter takes a more global perspective on how are perceptions are shaped and how we interact with one another.

The Building Blocks of Social Reality

From birth, you are enveloped in a multifaceted network of social structures and systems that scaffold your existence. Elements such as family, education, socioeconomic status, religion, media, and governance contribute uniquely to your social fabric, each adding a distinct shade of color to your reality palette.

While most of this chapter discusses how you are impacted by these global views, let's first start with your family. I don't have any siblings, and so it was very interesting for me to learn that two siblings can have very different parents. Depending on their parent's ages when they were born, the state of the world that impacted their parents beliefs, and the experiences they encountered throughout their lives. People evolve and change. Parents' evolve and change. The same two sisters can have very different fathers despite their shared biological DNA.

This notion of our evolution in thinking and behaviors is the same for each of us. Let's understand those influences.

As you navigate society's complex corridors, you absorb its unspoken rules, adopt its narratives, and wear its cultural glasses. Your upbringing, experiences, and exposure to diverse perspectives paint the canvas of your worldview. You inherit beliefs, biases, and societal norms that guide how you perceive yourself, others, and the world at large.

Aristotle said, "Man is by nature a social animal," highlighting the profound influence society has on individuals.

Your worldviews aren't self-formed; they are nurtured and shaped by the social contexts you live in and the experiences that you expose yourself to. Thus, it is key to expose yourself to different cultures and experiences if you want to expand your worldview.

For instance, consider a work setting. You may feel reluctant to attend a sensitivity training session, an unconscious bias workshop, or the upcoming discrimination or harassment seminar. You might argue that you've attended them before, that they aren't mandated by your state, or that they take precious time away from your work. "I'm a good person, and I always aim to do the right thing," you might say. And while most of us indeed have good intentions, we often overlook how our worldviews can unconsciously influence and shape our interactions with others. Awareness of your biases and preconceived notions is the first step toward more empathetic and understanding communication.

Examining the Threads: Social Norms and Influential Figures

This societal influence is glaringly evident in social norms. These unwritten rules form societal beliefs about acceptable behavior, guiding actions and shaping our assumptions of 'normalcy.' For instance, different societal views on gender roles profoundly impact individuals' perceptions and expectations in various cultures.

The words of influential figures also sway social norms and public beliefs. Regrettably, it is common for an influential person's personal beliefs to be interpreted as universal truths, which can often narrow understanding. The voices you attend to—be they business tycoons, media icons, or political leaders—hold enormous sway over our collective societal understanding.

Take the influence of tech leaders like Elon Musk or Mark Zuckerberg. Their voices bear substantial weight, and their views on technology's societal role have shaped public opinion and policy. However, their perspectives, while valid, aren't universally applicable. Conflating personal worldviews with universal truths risks erasing diverse experiences and perspectives that make up our complex society.

The Role of Media

Media is another potent societal influence. Various platforms, from newspapers to social media, significantly impact your understanding of the world around you. The media often acts as information gatekeepers, controlling news coverage, story framing, and public attention. The narratives you encounter through these media outlets actively shape your perceptions of the world.

Consider public opinion on immigration, a subject that elicits strong opinions and is often used as a political tool to garner support. Media portrayal dramatically sways views, producing a wide spectrum of perceptions that frame immigrants as either valuable contributors to society or

potential threats. Notably, these viewpoints often remain confined within the borders of one's own country, heavily influenced by media narratives and political campaigns.

Consequently, during public discussions on immigration, we often find ourselves parroting these sources instead of conducting our own research. Engaging with international comparisons of immigration policies, understanding the universal declaration of human rights laws, and assessing the short and long-term impacts of immigration on a country or community can offer a more rounded perspective on the issue.

In today's digital age, information is abundant, but the risk of echo chambers, spaces where only agreeable opinions are entertained, is real. Chapter seven highlights these dangers and the implications of limiting exposure to diverse perspectives.

"People's perceptions of reality will develop through their social networks and everyone will perceive that the information their social network produces reflects reality, but at the macro level, we will see an ever diverging cacophony of socially constructed realities."[2]

The Power of Education

Societal influences also originate from educational systems. The content we're taught, values imparted by educators, and the overall structure of educational institutions significantly impact a student's worldview.

For instance, education can mold young minds on global issues like climate change and inequality. Curriculums emphasizing environmental stewardship, sustainability, and global citizenship yield students likely to show a deeper understanding of these issues and the necessity of international cooperation.

Societal institutions like schools have a lasting impact on your worldviews. Your perceptions of global issues often stem from the education you receive. Recognizing this empowers you to critically examine these perspectives and seek more diverse knowledge sources.

Society undoubtedly shapes your worldviews in countless ways, often without you even realizing it. Recognizing these influences is the first step towards critically examining your worldviews and understanding their origins.

As you step into the societal dance that continually shapes your perceptions, embrace introspection. This is an opportunity to critically examine the societal lenses through which you view the world and consider whether they might need readjusting.

It's important to recognize that while your individual threads contribute to society's grand tapestry, they are also subtly influenced by it.

Now, it's time for action. Engage with diverse cultural experiences, participate in community initiatives, challenge biases, and empathize with marginalized communities. As you become aware of these external influences, you are then empowered to question, analyze, and adjust your perspectives.

Chapter 6 Action Items

* **Engage in diverse cultural experiences**: Visit cultural festivals, and museums, or try different cuisines.

* **Participate in community initiatives**: Get involved in volunteer work that promotes inclusivity and understanding across diverse cultural and social groups.

* **Challenge stereotypes** by actively seek out narratives, books, or films featuring underrepresented voices.

* **Enroll in unconscious bias training** to better understand the blindspots in your worldview.

Remember, we don't exist in isolation. As a part of a richly diverse, globally interconnected society, it's our collective responsibility to ensure that every thread in the tapestry is valued and appreciated for its unique contribution.

CHAPTER 7

Deconstructing Echo Chambers

In Chapter 6, we introduced the concept of echo chambers – environments where the same ideas, beliefs, and perspectives get repeated and amplified, often drowning out dissenting voices. Echo chambers occur naturally because of trust building and human experience, but they significantly shape our collective understanding and perception of reality.

Let's consider some common scenarios that foster these echo chambers. Within academic disciplines, for example, scholars form communities to exchange ideas and findings. While this leads to in-depth discussions and the advancement of knowledge, it may limit exposure to alternative perspectives.

Similarly, homogeneous neighborhoods and residential segregation contribute to the formation of echo chambers. When communities are predominantly composed of individuals from similar socioeconomic, cultural, or racial backgrounds, there is a higher likelihood of shared perspectives and limited exposure to diverse viewpoints. This can hinder cross-cultural understanding and perpetuate stereotypes and biases.

Support groups, such as those for individuals dealing with specific health conditions or life challenges, can also create a type of echo chamber. These groups provide a sense of belonging and offer a safe space for sharing experiences, receiving support, and exchanging advice. While the support is valuable, it is important for individuals to seek diverse perspectives and professional guidance to ensure a comprehensive understanding of their situation.

Echo Chambers in the Digital Age

Echo chambers have become especially prevalent within social media and online platforms. Thanks to design and algorithms that intuitively cater to users' existing preferences, these platforms create information silos that bolster confirmation bias and limit exposure to differing views. Individuals often find themselves surrounded by information that aligns with their existing beliefs.

This confinement restricts our exposure to conflicting perspectives, affecting critical thinking and the willingness to consider alternative viewpoints. This resistance has lasting implications for fostering productive and inclusive dialogue.

As discussed in Chapter 1, the unintended consequences of social media present a dilemma that warrants careful thought and conscious moderation. While social media platforms have the potential to amplify certain narratives and create filter bubbles, remember that you have agency in how you navigate and engage with these platforms.

You alone have the power and responsibility to vigilantly manage your own online experiences. By engaging in thoughtful and intentional online interactions, you can shape your own digital environment and safeguard yourself against the potential pitfalls of echo chambers and misinformation.

It's important to note that monitoring and moderating your relationship with social media does not mean suppressing freedom of speech or shutting yourself off from the digital world. Rather, it entails cultivating a healthy and discerning approach to the information you consume, actively seeking out diverse perspectives, and embracing critical thinking. Consider leveraging the benefits of these tools without allowing them to control your experiences.

Finding Echo Chambers in Traditional Media

Before the advent of social media, traditional media outlets also played a role in shaping public opinion. Biases—deliberate or unintentional—within these outlets could lead to the formation of echo chambers, where certain viewpoints or narratives were disproportionately represented or neglected. This lack of diverse perspectives hindered the exchange of ideas and influenced public discourse.

These platforms, which are often seen as trusted sources of information, held influence over public understanding and reporters, being human, were not always objective. When

objective facts become intertwined with personal opinions and storytelling angles, it could lead to skewed public opinion.

The Potential Consequences of Echo Chambers

Echo chambers are not inherently negative. They "may well be part of one's best strategy for maintaining a healthy access to truth-tracking evidence."[3]

Echo chambers, while potentially serving as spaces for support and community-building, can also lead to belief

polarization, which begins to erode the value of public discourse. Belief polarization amplifies the acceptance of belief as truth, as discussed in Chapter Four, widening the divide between individuals, and hindering our collective ability to bridge gaps and find common ground.

The impact of echo chambers and belief polarization on significant events like elections highlights its potentially detrimental effects on society. Political ideologies and affiliations often create scenarios where individuals primarily interact with like-minded individuals and consume news and information that aligns with their beliefs. These sources reinforce existing biases and limit exposure to alternative viewpoints, leading to further polarization within society.

The already divisive nature of politics can be further aggravated within virtual silos, pushing people towards extremism and hampering open, respectful discussion. In such scenarios, understanding the world in a way that allows you to make decisions becomes fragmented and narrowed down to your particular corners of reality.

An illustrative example of this is the 2016 U.S. Presidential Election. Research showed that in the weeks leading up to the election, people on either side of the political spectrum were rarely exposed to opinions from the other side on their social media feeds. The echo chambers formed within these online spaces resulted in increased polarization.

Echo Chambers in the Business World: Decision-Making Under Influence

Just as in social contexts, echo chambers can form in business environments and significantly impact decision-making processes. In this section, we will explore how echo chambers can influence business decisions and what steps can be taken to counteract these effects.

Echo chambers in business often emerge when leadership teams lack diversity. When leadership consists of individuals with similar backgrounds, perspectives, and experiences, there is a higher likelihood of

groupthink, a phenomenon where the desire for harmony and conformity within a group leads to irrational and dysfunctional decision-making. This lack of diversity can lead to narrow-minded decisions that fail to account for a broader range of perspectives and potential impacts.

Customer Perception and Market Understanding

Businesses that unknowingly exist within an echo chamber can miss key insights about their customers and markets.

By only focusing on information that aligns with their existing beliefs about their customer base, businesses can overlook crucial trends, fail to innovate, and end up out of touch with their customers' real needs and wants.

My business CauseLabs is a Public Benefit Corporation and a Certified B Corp. There was no market trend or key insights that led to this decision. Instead, it was a reflection of our values and how we wanted to align our operational decisions that guided us towards this specific business model. That said, our customers' perception of our company from our stories, our marketing, our operational decisions, etc. is one built on the values we care about most. For the most part, this has created favorable

perceptions of our brand, but it has also impacted us negatively when a company believes that we only work with nonprofits and dismisses the thought of working with our team.

Despite driving my stake in the ground to align my company with my purpose, I still cast a wide net for my ongoing learning so that I can see beyond the scope of our current work and business trends and can pivot as needed to serve clients and our community at large.

Influence of Industry Norms and Competitive Blindness

Echo chambers can also form around industry norms, leading businesses to unconsciously follow what competitors are doing rather than innovating or differentiating their offerings. This can create a market of similar products, stifling innovation and making businesses vulnerable to disruptive newcomers who can think outside the industry echo chamber.

To mitigate the potential impact of echo chambers on our business decisions, we can cultivate diversity at all levels of the company, encourage open dialogue, challenge existing ideas, and continuously seek out varied perspectives. Our businesses can also benefit from techniques such as scenario planning, which forces the consideration of various possible future situations, and red teaming, where a group is tasked with challenging any prevailing assumptions and the status quo. For businesses who practice EOS (the Entrepreneurial Operating System), one of the practices is to remember that there are no sacred cows, meaning that the way it has always been done can and likely should change if it is deemed good for the business and good for the customers.

By acknowledging the existence of echo chambers in business we can take proactive steps to counteract their influence.

Dismantling Echo Chambers

As you can see, echo chambers particularly in the age of technology can present a significant challenge in your endeavor to broaden perspectives. Despite these challenges, there have been instances where individuals and communities have successfully dismantled echo chambers. Initiatives like bridge-building conversations, exposure to different viewpoints, collaborative projects and initiatives, and education and awareness campaigns have proven effective.

* Bridge-building conversations: Within diverse communities and organizations, bridge-building conversations have been initiated to link individuals of differing ideologies. These dialogues promote understanding, enabling participants to share experiences, challenge assumptions, and find shared interests.

* Exposure to different viewpoints: Many individuals actively seek diverse information sources, challenging their existing beliefs by engaging with varied perspectives. This deliberate exposure broadens their understanding, promotes critical thinking, and contributes to a more nuanced worldview.

* Collaborative projects and initiatives: Collaborative projects uniting diverse individuals effectively dismantle echo chambers by confronting biases and fostering constructive dialogue. These collaborations value diverse perspectives, promote shared purpose, and build more inclusive communities.

* Education and awareness campaigns: Initiatives launched by various entities promote media literacy, critical thinking, and echo chamber awareness. These campaigns stress seeking diverse perspectives, fact-checking, and understanding social media's role in shaping reality. Such efforts empower individuals with essential knowledge, fostering a more informed society.

These efforts emphasize the power of human agency in dismantling echo chambers. By seeking out diverse perspectives, engaging in dialogue, and challenging your own biases, you can break free from the confines of echo chambers and foster a more empathetic and open-minded society.

Chapter 7 Action Items

As you continue to explore ways to expand your perspectives, here are some action items to consider:

* **Audit your social media** feeds and intentionally diversify your sources of information.

* **Engage in respectful and constructive conversations** and listen for common ground to bridge the gap between differing perspectives.

* **Seek out podcasts or online forums** that encourage healthy discussions across ideological divides.

* **Practice critical thinking by fact-checking** information and be mindful of echo chambers in online communities.

* **Use the power of AI**. While AI may be biased by the influence of its trainers, there is a wealth of data and you can use this provide you with critiques, contrary views, or highlight gaps in your thinking.

In the next chapter, we'll discuss how experiencing diverse social interactions can provide a more comprehensive understanding of our shared reality.

Remember, while echo chambers are a natural outcome of your social interactions, both in real life and online, you can strive to step outside of these boxes to expand your views and combat the influence of limiting or potentially harmful silos.

CHAPTER 8

CHAPTER 8

Broadening Our Perspective

Given the influence and limitations of personal perspectives and societal echo chambers, how can we expand our point of view? This chapter explores ways to broaden perspectives, namely through travel, reading, engaging with different cultures, and seeking diverse social interactions. The benefits of these actions are manifold: they foster empathy, challenge assumptions, and broaden our worldview.

The Journey of Travel: A Personal Perspective

Individuals who engage in immersive travel experiences share stories of significant shifts in their perspectives.

Psychologist Todd B. Kashdan believes that travel should be routinely used to "get out of your comfort zone, expose yourself to uncertainty, and eschew rest for exploration and learning. The result is personal growth — greater emotional agility, empathy, and creativity."

Raised as an immigrant child in a military family, I was very fortunate to be exposed at a young age to cultural diversity. This early exposure instilled in me a sense of open-mindedness and a willingness to embrace different perspectives.

In my thirties, I took a work trip to India. During my trip, I had a deep reconnection with experiences that mirrored my childhood. While my memories and experiences had

always been present, the journey in India unearthed a deeper understanding of my own poverty story.

This revelation not only expanded my understanding of the forces that shaped my worldview but also deepened my appreciation for the work I do, inspiring me to make conscious choices that positively impact both people and the environment.

Whether through travel that broadens your horizons or, like in my case, rediscovering a part of your own personal story, the immersion into different ways of life while traveling globally holds the power to connect us despite of our differences. These experiences become invaluable contributions to the tapestry of 'The World We Know,' enriching our understanding of humanity and encouraging us to make a positive difference in the lives of others.

To embrace the unknown while traveling, consider exploring without a preplanned itinerary, allowing yourself the space for spontaneous discovery.

Reading: A Passport to Diverse Perspectives

Reading introduces us to countless worlds and interesting perspectives. The narratives we encounter in books invite us to explore unfamiliar landscapes, meet diverse characters, and grapple with complex themes.

For those who are passionate readers, you may have fond memories of participating in your local library's summer reading program. One particular community reading program I had the pleasure of experiencing was a captivating scavenger hunt, where I embarked on an adventure throughout time, searching for the artifacts hidden within the pages of various stories.

Reading, in essence, becomes a passport to countless worlds, extending an open invitation to see the world through the eyes of others. It is within the realm of books that understanding expands, biases are challenged, and the capacity for compassion is ignited.

"A reader lives a thousand lives before he dies. The man who never reads lives only one."

GEORGE R.R. MARTIN

Each page presents an opportunity for imagination and transformation. By immersing in the written word, you embark on a personal odyssey of growth, forging connections with the hearts and minds of individuals who may originate from different cultures, backgrounds, and life experiences.

As previously highlighted, the embrace of diverse cultural perspectives can serve as a wellspring of creativity and fuel innovation, particularly in the context of fostering a diverse workforce. However, it is essential to recognize that the expansion of perspectives can begin at an early age, and one powerful avenue for this growth is through the act of reading.

Dr. Rudine Sims Bishop offers a captivating analogy in her insightful work "Mirrors, Windows, and Sliding Glass

Doors," underscoring the significance of diversity in early childhood literature. She asserts that "window books remind readers that their view is not the only view," emphasizing the vital need for diversity to flow in both directions. She astutely observes that when children exclusively encounter mirrors in books, they develop a distorted perception of the world, as the world itself is becoming increasingly colorful and diverse with the passage of time.[4]

Reading broadens your horizons, nurtures your curiosity, and creates a sense of interconnectedness with the vast tapestry of human existence. It is through the act of reading that you discover the power of words to weave your worldview.

Cultural Immersion: Fostering Empathy and Understanding

Engaging in immersive cultural experiences, whether through travel or local activities is known to cultivating empathy and understanding towards individuals from different backgrounds.

A remarkable example of this transformative effect is evident in a group of volunteers who participated in a community development project in a rural village. Their firsthand onsite experience shattered stereotypes and left them with a richer appreciation for human diversity.

Cultural immersion acts as a powerful tool in dismantling the walls of prejudice, revealing the depths of our shared humanity while highlighting that our commonalities far surpass our differences.

Cultural immersion can be encouraged from a young age through international school exchange programs. By actively supporting and engaging youth in these opportunities, we nurture a generation that embraces and values cross-cultural experiences and foster a sense of interconnectedness.

Adults can engage with local community organizations, non-profit groups, language schools, and cultural centers that promote cultural exchange and understanding.

Remember, cultural immersion is not limited to international experiences. Engaging with diverse communities within your own locality can also provide valuable opportunities for cross-cultural interactions and learning. Stay curious and be open to new experiences. Such experiences pave the way for a more connected society, where empathy and appreciation for human diversity are celebrated as fundamental pillars of our collective progress.

Diverse Social Interactions: Embracing Cross-Cultural Dialogue

Diverse social interactions offer a powerful avenue for personal growth and societal progress. Actively engaging in meaningful conversations with those from diverse cultural, socioeconomic, and ideological backgrounds, and who may hold opposing views from your own promotes mutual respect and social cohesion. This helps foster a society that thrives on diverse perspectives.

To act, you can initiate conversations with individuals who possess different skills and abilities, life experiences, or religious beliefs. Actively listen and empathize with their experiences. This can be done through community events, social gatherings, or joining discussion groups focused on promoting diverse viewpoints. It is important to approach these interactions with an open mind, curiosity, and a genuine willingness to understand and learn from others. Seeking diverse perspectives in your personal and professional life allows you to see beyond your personal experiences and the societal echo chambers you inhabit.

Chapter 8 Action Items

Here's a recap of action items to consider:

* **Actively seek out opportunities for cultural exchange**, such as participating in language exchange programs or attending international events.

* **Watch documentaries** that expose you to different cultures, traditions, and historical contexts.

* **Engage in intercultural dialogue** by participating in workshops, discussion groups, or online platforms that facilitate conversations with individuals from diverse backgrounds.

* **Challenge your own biases** and assumptions by reflecting on how cultural values and norms may shape your worldview.

In the next chapter, we'll step into embracing the unknown, an essential aspect of broadening our worldviews.

CHAPTER 9

Embracing the Unknown

You have traversed 'The World We Know,' uncovering that your perspectives and truths are constructed from numerous external and internal influences, often subconsciously. We now arrive at an essential question: How can you confront and relinquish your fear or resistance to the unknown, opening yourself to boundless growth and potential?

Embracing the unknown requires summoning the courage to accept uncertainty and detach yourself from rigid outcomes. You must face your fears directly and welcome novel experiences, thoughts, and ideas. This path requires you to step away from the comfort of your established beliefs and expand your understanding through the lens of others.

> *"We strive toward knowledge, always more knowledge, but must understand that we are, and will remain, surrounded by mystery."*
>
> MARCELO GLEISER

Renowned theoretical physicist Marcelo Gleiser echoes this sentiment, "We strive toward knowledge, always more knowledge, but must understand that we are, and will remain, surrounded by mystery."

Courage in Uncertainty: The Power of Healthy Detachment

At a workshop I attended, aptly named 'The Courage Map,' Franziska Iseli recounted personal stories that stuck with me. In one of her stories, she shared how unexpected travel mishaps pushed her out of her comfort zone, compelling her to embrace uncertainty and let go of her meticulously laid plans.

These were not minor mishaps either, which is perhaps what drew me into empathizing with the emotional state she must have been feeling at the time. She had ridden her motorcycle across the country only to discover that she had the wrong paperwork to cross the border. In the telling of her story, I could feel her disappointment in those moments.

Franziska goes on to recount her less planned and yet, still incredible experiences. She now shares that it takes great courage to detach from our desired outcomes. I believe this is true for so many instances in our lives including goals, conversations, decisions, and even the unfolding of events.

I found it inspiring that this newfound courage, coupled with a generous dose of humility, didn't just stop at her travel experiences—it permeated other facets of her life, including her business ventures. To me, this ability to adapt and persevere in the face of the unknown exemplifies resilience—a skill that I believe is vital in navigating life's unpredictable twists and turns.

The Role of Curiosity and Humility

At the heart of embracing the unknown lies the indispensable trait of curiosity. As Albert Einstein astutely observed, "I have no special talent. I am only passionately curious." His claim suggests that intense curiosity compels you to question, explore, and tirelessly seek understanding. Harnessing your innate sense of curiosity catalyzes personal growth, challenges assumptions, and leads to transformative journeys beyond your comfort zone.

Reflecting on the story of Dr. Jane Goodall, a celebrated primatologist and anthropologist, we witness the power of curiosity in action. Goodall's curiosity about animals and their behaviors led her into the forests of Gombe. Despite having no formal training at the time, her observations revolutionized everyone's understanding of primates, challenging established scientific beliefs and contributing invaluable knowledge to the field.

But curiosity alone is not enough. Embracing the unknown also requires humility—recognizing that your knowledge and understanding are always incomplete and that there's always more to learn.

Chinese philosopher Confucius stated, "Real knowledge is to know the extent of one's ignorance." This insight encapsulates the essence of exploration and discovery;

acknowledging the limitations of your understanding can propel you toward deeper knowledge.

Fostering the Pursuit of Knowledge

In the spirit of Confucius' wisdom, we come to realize that true wisdom is not about claiming to possess all the answers, but rather acknowledging the boundless territories of knowledge that remain unexplored. This understanding ignites our curiosity and humility, fostering continuous learning and growth.

As you embrace the unknown, akin to historic explorers, embark on intellectual expeditions, driven by a thirst for knowledge and a desire to decipher the world's mysteries. Leave the comfort of the known and journey into uncharted territories, discovering new horizons of understanding and revealing the immensity of what awaits discovery.

Thus, embrace Confucius's wisdom as an invitation to venture into knowledge and understanding, guided by curiosity, humility, and an unwavering commitment to expanding your intellectual boundaries.

Comfort in Uncertainty and Embracing Continuous Learning

Becoming comfortable with uncertainty creates opportunities for breakthroughs and progress. This principle resonates deeply with the scientific method, where hypotheses are formed, tested, and refined, acknowledging that conclusions are always subject to revision considering new evidence.

In essence, embracing the unknown is more than seeking all the answers; it's a mindset that nurtures openness, persistent questioning, and an eagerness to learn from diverse perspectives. It is the practice of letting go of outcomes, and perhaps, recognizing that there is more than one path.

For fans of the multiverse, perhaps you can teach me how to experience every path simultaneously. I haven't cracked that nut.

All joking aside, there is tremendous potential to unlock different areas of our brain and to learn differently. I'm a big fan of Carol Dweck, the author of 'Mindset'. Her lessons on fostering a growth mindset is something that I have used for years both personally and professionally. It's amazing what life-changing technology has emerged from infusing our team with the growth mindset and creating space and culture for it within our company.

"Picture your brain forming new connections as you meet the challenge and learn. Keep on going."

CAROL DWECK

This approach recognizes that 'The World We Know' is a dynamic entity, constantly evolving, and with those shifts, your understanding of it must evolve in sync.

As you navigate through the ever-unfolding complexities of life, embrace uncertainties, for within them lie the seeds of discovery and growth. Stay curious, resilient, and open-minded, driven by the pursuit of knowledge and the yearning to unveil new layers of understanding. By embracing the unknown, you transcend your limitations, reaching a little closer to enlightenment.

Chapter 9 Action Items

* **Cultivate curiosity**: Nurture your innate sense of curiosity by asking questions, seeking new knowledge, and exploring unfamiliar topics.

* **Step out of your comfort zone**: Challenge yourself to try new experiences and embrace uncertainty. This can be anything from playing with your young children and seeing the world through their eyes, to flying a plane and seeing the world from a different perspective.

* **Practice mindfulness**: Develop a mindset of openness and acceptance, being present in the moment, and releasing the need for control.

* **Embrace lifelong learning**: Adopt a growth mindset and commit to continuous learning and personal development, acknowledging that the journey of understanding and discovery is an ongoing process.

As you venture into the realms of the unknown, remember that personal growth lies not in the destination, but in the journey itself. Embrace this mindset with an open mind, relentless curiosity, and an insatiable thirst for knowledge. By adopting this approach, you can unlock new possibilities and expand your understanding.

Next we will explore how you can translate your expanded understanding of 'The World We Know' into actions that radiate kindness, compassion, and faith in humanity.

CHAPTER 10

A Beacon For Humanity's Future

In my quest to understand 'The World We Know,' I stood at a pivotal junction. I had the choice to remain confined within the boundaries of my personal perspectives and societal echo chambers or venture down the path of compassion and empathy, reshaping my world in the process. Writing this book has been a hike along the latter path. I admit that I don't know the final destination, but I've experienced positive changes in my personal habits along the way.

Some of these changes for the better were not immediately accepted as normal. In fact, not being as emotional during conversations where I know I would have been emotional in the past initially left me questioning whether something was wrong with me.

I was accustomed to expressing emotions in a certain way during conversations, usually getting very upset if I was not being understood. When that changed, it felt like a deviation from my usual self. However, as I've grown and reflected upon these changes, I've come to realize that they are a healthy part of my personal growth journey.

Through sharing these insights, I hope you can also gain value and inspiration. This final chapter presents a compelling case for embracing a more holistic and inclusive worldview, one that embraces the multitude of perspectives and truths that coexist in our diverse society. By doing so, you not only contribute to the creation of a harmonious society but also unlock transformative benefits across various aspects of your life, including your relationships, businesses, self-perception, and overall well-being.

Bridging Divides: The Parable of the Good Samaritan

Let's consider the parable of the Good Samaritan, a timeless tale from the Gospel of Luke. This story underscores the virtues of compassion, empathy, and selflessly helping others in need.

In the parable, a Jewish man is robbed, beaten, and left for dead while traveling. Several passersby, including figures of religious prominence, avoid the injured man. However, a Samaritan—whose people were historically shunned by the Jewish community—comes across him. Ignoring societal divides, the Samaritan feels compassion for the man, tends to his wounds, and ensures his care and comfort at an inn.

The parable of the Good Samaritan illustrates the lesson that true compassion knows no boundaries. It urges us to look past societal divisions, prejudices, and personal biases, and extend help to anyone in need, regardless of their background. The story serves as a reminder that we all have the capacity to bridge divides, heal wounds, and bring about positive change in our world.

Nurturing Relationships and Driving Innovation: The Impact of Empathy and Diversity

In our all of our relationships, embracing empathy and understanding nurtures deeper connections and fosters effective communication. By genuinely stepping into another person's shoes and seeing the world through their eyes, we can better resolve conflicts and strengthen the bonds that unite us.

Research conducted at the University of Cambridge affirms the significance of empathy in romantic relationships. Couples who demonstrate high levels of empathy towards each other report greater satisfaction in their partnership.

When we extend this understanding of empathy to all our relationships—be they familial, romantic, or platonic—we recognize the immense value of diverse perspectives and the richness they bring to our interpersonal connections.

Beyond personal relationships, an inclusive worldview holds tremendous potential in driving innovation and growth within businesses. Studies consistently show that diverse teams outperform homogeneous teams by leveraging a multitude of perspectives, ideas, and problem-solving approaches. McKinsey's research highlights that businesses with greater racial and ethnic diversity are 35% more likely to have financial success, further reinforcing the importance of diversity in our organizational contexts.[5]

Embracing Our Unique Journeys: The Beauty of Individual Perspectives

Our worldview significantly shapes our self-perception and overall happiness. When we acknowledge that multiple realities coexist, we free ourselves from the constraints of conforming to a singular norm. We learn to embrace our unique journeys, fostering self-acceptance and nurturing a positive self-image.

In the words of Malcolm Forbes, Entrepreneur and founder of Forbes magazine, "Diversity: the art of thinking independently together." This powerful statement underlines the essence of unity through diversity, reminding us that our differences enrich the human tapestry rather than divide us.

Embracing Change and Moving Forward: The Call to Action

Our exploration of 'The World We Know' serves as our call to action—an invitation to celebrate diversity, venture beyond our echo chambers, and expand our horizons. It urges us to recognize our differences as enriching elements rather than sources of division. With empathy, compassion, and understanding, we become agents of positive change, building better together and creating a brighter future for everyone.

Chapter 10 Action Items

Let's engage in some actionable steps towards a more unified future.

* **Cultivate empathy & understanding**: Join an empathetic listening workshop. Actively listen to others. Seek to understand others' before being understood. Above all, practice kindness and compassion.

* **Embrace diversity**: Celebrate the richness of diversity in all forms, valuing different perspectives, and fostering

inclusivity in your personal and professional relationships.

* **Promote and advocate for positive change**: Engage in activities that support social justice, equality, and inclusion, making a positive impact on your community and the world.

* **Foster self-acceptance**: Acknowledge and value your unique experiences and truths, promoting self-acceptance and embracing your authentic self. When you recognize an existing bias, give yourself grace and then, seek to understand and grow.

As you venture into an era marked by unprecedented diversity and interconnectedness, remember that you play an integral part in shaping the future you want to see. Through empathy, understanding, and action, you can foster unity, promote understanding, and pave the way toward more meaningful connections.

CHAPTER 11

Shaping Our Collective World

We conclude our exploration of 'The World We Know,' grounded in an essential realization: the world isn't a monolithic, uniform entity. Instead, it is a vibrant mosaic, filled with a myriad of perspectives, experiences, and truths. Embracing this multiplicity is the crucial first step toward nurturing a society imbued with compassion, empathy, and understanding.

In this book, you've opened the door to the labyrinth of perception, investigating how individual truths mold your shared reality, and scrutinizing the dangers of insular echo chambers. We've illuminated the transformative potential of expanding your perspectives and comprehending the ramifications of your actions on others and our shared environment.

Embracing Change: The Path Ahead

But why does all this matter? This understanding is essential in our current era, a period teeming with unprecedented challenges and rapid changes in social structures and in technology. Recent global events have exposed deep divides and amplified the cry for change.

The COVID-19 pandemic, in particular, laid bare the interconnectedness of our global community and underlined the importance of unity when tackling shared challenges. It has urged us to prioritize cooperation in building a more resilient and sustainable future while highlighting the individual responsibility each of us bears.

While it's a popular quote, times of crisis often resurface and echo Mahatma Gandhi's words, "Be the change that you wish to see in the world."

Stepping into the Shoes of Others

If we remain divided, waiting for others to initiate change, our shared problems will only grow heavier and appear increasingly overwhelming. Each of us holds a responsibility to act, not only for our own well-being but for the betterment of everyone. In 'The World We Know,' I emphasize the importance of appreciating and celebrating the diverse spectrum of human experiences, as it is through this understanding that we can shape a world that authentically reflects our collective identities. It all begins with recognizing and embracing our own unique perspectives and truths. As you work through the action items, you will notice that there are many activities that ask us to work on ourselves first, but also the soft skills of active listening and empathy are key to understanding the world beyond our comfort zones.

I vividly recall an experience that broadened my perspective. In 2022, I had the opportunity to attend a Dine in the Dark event with Jeremy Poincenot, a remarkable individual who began losing his eyesight at a young age.

Despite this challenge, Jeremy not only persevered but also became a professional golfer and an inspirational speaker. As I sat blindfolded, navigating my way through the meal, I encountered the difficulties and challenges that Jeremy faces daily.

However, what truly struck me was not the physical obstacles of cutting through asparagus or finding my drink. The most significant struggle arose from filtering out noise and focusing on the conversation at my table without the visual cues of eye contact, lip-reading, and facial expressions.

That experience illustrates the struggle and hesitation we feel when venturing beyond our comfort zones. We often find reasons to resist and revert to what is familiar. But for Jeremy Poincenot, there was no choice. His eyesight was not improving, and he had to adapt. This experience served as a powerful reminder of the transformative potential that lies within us when we are willing to embrace discomfort and challenge our preconceived notions.

If our divisions continue to cause irreparable harm to ourselves and those around us, we must reflect on the right course of action. What would you change if you had no choice? What level of discomfort are you willing to accept in order to forge meaningful connections and move toward a more interconnected world? These questions, rooted in personal experience and shared humanity, ask you to examine your role in shaping the path ahead.

The Journey Continues

Our journey towards a better world isn't limited to the confines of this book. It represents a continuous process of discovery, growth, and collective action. Each of us holds an invaluable part in shaping the world we want.

To quote renowned astrophysicist, Neil deGrasse Tyson, "We are all connected; To each other, biologically. To the Earth, chemically. To the rest of the universe atomically." Leverage this profound interconnectedness to shape a world that celebrates our shared humanity. You can become a catalyst for positive change, a champion for understanding, and the architect of a better future.

As you close this book, remember that the world as I understand it, and the world as you comprehend it, will continue to exist. However, it is my fervent hope that together, we can forge a shared understanding of 'The World We Know.'

*"We are all connected; To each other,
biologically. To the Earth, chemically. To
the rest of the universe atomically."*

NEIL DEGRASSE TYSON

APPENDIX

1. Chapter 3. Information on the study related to the Pygmalion Effect: https://files.eric.ed.gov/fulltext/EJ1066376.pdf

2. Chapter 6. Social networks' effect on reality: Wohn and Bowe, 2014 (https://www.researchgate.net/publication/262365850_Crystallization_How_social_media_facilitates_social_construction_of_reality#:~:text=...,Wohn%20and%20Bowe%2C%202014)

3. Chapter 8. A quote about echo chambers: Cambridge University Press. (https://www.cambridge.org/core/journals/episteme/article/from-belief-polarization-to-echo-chambers-a-rationalizing-account/FCC9AB2691CD160F53BB904C128DD81D#)

4. Chapter 8. Dr. Rudine Sims Bishop's work about Mirrors, Windows, and Sliding Glass Doors: Color in Colorado - 'Why Diverse Books Matter' (https://www.colorincolorado.org/article/why-diverse-books-matter-mirrors-and-windows)

5. Chapter 10. Workplace diversity data: McKinsey - Why Diversity Matters (https://www.mckinsey.com/capabilities/people-and-organizational-performance/our-insights/why-diversity-matters)

ALL ACTION ITEMS BY CHAPTER

I hope you have found value in this exploration into "The World We Know." Here's a quick guide to all of the action items by chapter.

Chapter 1

Reflect on how your perception of reality may have been shaped by your experiences and influences.

Chapter 2

Explore how team competitions and social constructs have influenced your behaviors and your views of others.

Challenge your assumptions by seeking out alternative sources of information and exposing yourself to diverse viewpoints.

Chapter 3

Engage in perspective-taking exercises, such as writing from the point of view of someone with opposing beliefs.

Seek out diverse sources of information including books, articles, podcasts, and documentaries, to broaden your understanding of different perspectives.

Practice awareness of how your perspectives influence others. Also, recognize any feelings of discomfort and seek to understand the narratives that create these reactions. Surround yourself with people who positively influence your awareness and perspectives.

Chapter 4

Foster cognitive flexibility: Intentionally explore multiple perspectives on a given topic before forming your own opinion. This practice enhances your ability to grasp the complexity of truth.

Engage in respectful debates and discussions: Seek out opportunities to engage in conversations with others who hold opposing viewpoints. By understanding their perspectives, you can challenge your own beliefs and broaden your understanding.

Explore diverse narratives: Read books or articles that offer different perspectives on historical events or social issues. By exposing yourself to a range of viewpoints, you can gain a deeper appreciation for the multifaceted nature of truth and enhance your ability to engage in informed discussions.

Practice intellectual humility: Recognize the limitations of your own knowledge and remain open to the possibility of learning from others. Embracing intellectual humility allows you to approach discussions and disagreements with an open mind, fostering a spirit of curiosity and continuous learning.

Chapter 5

Reflect on the beliefs you hold as "truth" and critically examine the evidence and reasoning behind them.

Regularly expose yourself to diverse sources of information to challenge confirmation bias and broaden your understanding of complex issues. Converse with individuals who hold different beliefs and seek to understand their perspectives

Practice being open to revisiting your long-held beliefs when presented with new evidence or compelling arguments for deeper understanding.

Engage in diverse cultural experiences: Visit cultural festivals, and museums, or try different cuisines.

Participate in community initiatives: Get involved in volunteer work that promotes inclusivity and understanding across diverse cultural and social groups.

Challenge stereotypes by actively seek out narratives, books, or films featuring underrepresented voices.

Enroll in unconscious bias training to better understand the blindspots in your worldview.

Audit your social media feeds and intentionally diversify your sources of information.

Engage in respectful and constructive conversations and listen for common ground to bridge the gap between differing perspectives.

Seek out podcasts or online forums that encourage healthy discussions across ideological divides.

Practice critical thinking by fact-checking information and be mindful of echo chambers in online communities.

Use the power of AI. While AI may be biased by the influence of its trainers, there is a wealth of data and you can use this provide you with critiques, contrary views, or highlight gaps in your thinking.

Chapter 8

Actively seek out opportunities for cultural exchange, such as participating in language exchange programs or attending international events.

Watch documentaries that explore different cultures, traditions, and historical contexts.

Engage in intercultural dialogue by participating in workshops, discussion groups, or online platforms that facilitate conversations with individuals from diverse backgrounds.

Challenge your own biases and assumptions by reflecting on how cultural norms may shape your worldview.

Chapter 9

Cultivate curiosity: Nurture your innate sense of curiosity by asking questions, seeking new knowledge, and exploring unfamiliar topics.

Step out of your comfort zone: Challenge yourself to try new experiences and embrace uncertainty. This can be anything from playing with your young children and seeing the world through their eyes, to flying a plane and seeing the world from a different perspective.

Practice mindfulness: Develop a mindset of openness and acceptance, being present in the moment, and releasing the need for control.

Embrace lifelong learning: Adopt a growth mindset and commit to continuous learning and personal development, acknowledging that the journey of understanding and discovery is an ongoing process.

Chapter 10

Cultivate empathy & understanding: Join an empathetic listening workshop. Actively listen to others. Seek to understand others' before being understood. Above all, practice kindness and compassion.

Embrace diversity: Celebrate the richness of diversity in all forms, valuing different perspectives, and fostering inclusivity in your personal and professional relationships.

Promote and advocate for positive change: Engage in activities that support social justice, equality, and inclusion, making a positive impact on your community and the world.

Foster self-acceptance: Acknowledge and value your unique experiences and truths, promoting self-acceptance and embracing your authentic self. When you recognize an existing bias, give yourself grace and then, seek to understand and grow.

ABOUT THE AUTHOR

Sheryle Gillihan

Sheryle Gillihan is an esteemed leader, entrepreneur, and social impact advocate. As the co-owner and CEO of CauseLabs, a public benefit corporation based in Texas, she has demonstrated her commitment to using business and technology as forces for good and growing positive impact. With a career marked by innovation and purpose, Sheryle has garnered recognition for her exceptional leadership in the field of social impact.

Beyond her professional endeavors, Sheryle treasures her role as a wife and mother. She shares a loving partnership of over 25 years with her husband, Michael Gillihan, who serves as the co-owner and CTO/COO of CauseLabs. Together, they have raised two remarkable adult children, Max and Alli, nurturing a close-knit family unit.

Sheryle's journey began in the Philippines, where she was born into humble circumstances and raised by a single mother. Her life took a transformative turn when her father, a US Air Force Tech Sergeant at the time, returned from Korea and united their family, immigrating to the United States of America. Sheryle recognizes the privilege bestowed upon her as an American citizen, providing her with opportunities that her earlier circumstances would not have allowed. However, she keenly felt the weight of her mother's sacrifices and struggles, driving her to make the most of the opportunities afforded to her.

Inspired by influential figures such as Amina J. Mohammed and General Colin Powell, Sheryle understood the transformative power of her environment and harnessed it to fuel her personal and professional growth. Her experiences as a first-generation immigrant, married with her faith-led entrepreneurship, and her military experience both as a dependent and a soldier have shaped her perspectives and strengthened her resolve to make a difference in the world.

In her role as an author, Sheryle brings a unique blend of objectivity and personal connection. Drawing from her own experiences, observations, and aspirations, she weaves a narrative that speaks to the essence of her journey.

The topics explored in this book are intellectual endeavors and deeply personal expressions of her quest for understanding, empathy, and acceptance. Sheryle courageously shares true events, her own stories, and stories she has heard to provoke thought and inspire action.

Throughout this book, Sheryle emphasizes that her truth may differ from others, yet it is through these diverse perspectives that growth and transformation can occur. It is her earnest desire that this book catalyzes awareness, empathy, and acceptance—an urgent call to action for building a more compassionate and harmonious world.

For more information about Sheryle Gillihan and her impactful work, visit sherylegillihan.com, causelabs.com or find the Woman Owned Agency podcast on your preferred streaming platform.